MW01264579

COFFEE
THE LITTLE
EVERYTHING GUIDE

SETH MARTIN

© **Copyright 2017 by Seth Martin - All rights reserved.**

This document is geared towards providing exact and reliable information in regards to the topic and issue covered. The publication is sold with the idea that the publisher is not required to render accounting, officially permitted, or otherwise, qualified services. If advice is necessary, legal or professional, a practiced individual in the profession should be ordered.

- From a Declaration of Principles which was accepted and approved equally by a Committee of the American Bar Association and a Committee of Publishers and Associations.

In no way is it legal to reproduce, duplicate, or transmit any part of this document in either electronic means or in printed format. Recording of this publication is strictly prohibited and any storage of this document is not allowed unless with written permission from the publisher. All rights reserved.

The information provided herein is stated to be truthful and consistent, in that any liability, in terms of inattention or otherwise, by any usage or abuse of any policies, processes, or directions contained within is the solitary and utter responsibility of the recipient reader. Under no circumstances will any legal responsibility or blame be held against the publisher for any reparation, damages, or monetary loss due to the information herein, either directly or indirectly.

Respective authors own all copyrights not held by the publisher.

The information herein is offered for informational purposes solely, and is universal as so. The presentation of the information is without contract or any type of guarantee assurance.

The trademarks that are used are without any consent, and the publication of the trademark is without permission or backing by the trademark owner. All trademarks and brands within this book are for clarifying purposes only and are the owned by the owners themselves, not affiliated with this document.

Table of Contents

Introduction

I want to thank you and congratulate you for downloading the book, *"The Coffee Encyclopedia: A Comprehensive Guide To All Things Coffee A-Z List Of Drinks, Styles, Brews, Beans, And More"*.

This book has I eye-opening information about coffee. It provides an A-Z list of drinks, styles, brews, beans and much more to hopefully help you transform how you prepare, drink, smell, and buy coffee.

Coffee, the drink for the civilized folk, is one interesting beverage. The silky taste and the energy that comes with it is enough to make almost everyone fall for it. If you are already a mad coffee addict, then this book will be mad fun for you.

If you love coffee and ever been intimidated by the extensive vocabulary and variety in the world of coffee like I was once upon a time, then you like me wanted to consume not just the drink but the whole world into it. This book will give you the coffee literacy that you might so much desire to experiment with your next favorite drink or converse like a pro with your friends. It will show you all the fun ways that you can brew, drink, and style up your coffee. Whether you want to make cappuccino, café latte, or any other coffee brew that you only find in coffee shops, this book has an A-Z list of all that, as well as easy-to-follow steps that will help you make your very own cup of coffee at home—just the way you like it. Or spice up your usual coffee routine by trying out new coffee recipes or techniques from other parts of the world. There are many ways to enjoy coffee, and that just makes everything more fun. Cheers to coffee! Enjoy!

Thanks again for getting this book. I hope you enjoy it!

The History of Coffee and Its Cultural Role

"Coffee is a language in itself." —Jackie Chan, actor

Before we jump right into the A-Z list of coffee brews that you can make at home or order at your favorite shop, let's start by learning how coffee became what it is today, as well as its immense cultural footprint in today's society.

The History of Coffee

Coffee has been a part of human culture for thousands of years. It can only be grown in certain places but the history is not regional and has an interesting global voyage. The history of coffee officially dates back to the year 850—in Persia, however coffee has many references and legends about it that predate that.

One of the most interesting legendary tales from way back originates from the history of Islam. It tells how Angel Gabriel woke up Mohamed from slumber with a hot cup of coffee before he undertook a great task. The effect of the coffee was so strong that it helped the prophet rouse from sleep and gave him the energy he needed to defeat a horde of 40 men in just one battle!

In the Bible, there is also a reference to coffee described in the book of Kings in form of a 'roasted grain' that was offered to David.

However, the history of coffee seems to have begun in the Caffa region of Ethiopia in the late 6th century AD. The legend behind the discovery is that here, a goat herder named Kaldi noticed that his flock was restless and energetic after eating red berries and leaves from an unidentified shrub. The herder got curious and he ended up tasting the berries himself. He was so happy with the effects of the coffee such that he was spotted by monks dancing with his goats. The monks brought some fruit back to the monastery. They consumed the plant the same way the goats and Kaldi did, and spent the night awake and full of energy. Soon enough, the monks began boiling the berries themselves and drinking the liquid so that they could stay alert during their night ceremonies and long rituals.

Because of this stimulating characteristic, the use of coffee spread significantly among monasteries, and then it was taken to Yemen by the Ethiopian army. From here, the word and uses of coffee spread as far as the cities of Medina and Mecca—in fact, the Muslim pilgrims smuggled the plants to Mecca.

The stimulant beverage became popular among Muslims for the same reason that monks got hooked to it. It kept them up and awake during long sessions of worship and prayer. It is in Arabia where the modern method of roasting coffee beans started, during the 13th century.

The use of coffee continued to spread to all over the world through many pilgrims who visited the coffee-infused cities, tasted the coffee there for the first time, then took it back to their homelands. The Muslims called it 'qahwah', which was at first the romantic term for wine. The Turks called it 'qahve', the Dutch 'koffie', which later became caffe then café in the European lingo, and finally 'coffee' in the English language.

The Dutch were the ones who supplied the coffee plant itself to the world where they first brought it from Yemen (Mocha) to Holland in the year 1616. They conducted their first cultivation in 1658 in Sri Lanka, which was previously known as Ceylon.

Coffee reached Asia and Africa around the 16th century. Carried by traders, explorers, and pilgrims, coffee crawled its roots into the Middle East, India, Southeast Asia, and Africa, eventually spreading into Italy, France, and the rest of Europe, then finally to America, starting with Latin America.

The first coffeehouse in London was opened in the 17th century where afterwards, the coffee houses came to be known as 'Penny Universities'. This is because it was joked that you could get educated as you sip coffee for only 1 cent by just paying attention to all the great minds who voiced their opinions in the shops. Coffeehouses then spread from London to all around the world. One coffeehouse, which was the first of many, in Paris known as 'Le Procope' is still operating now!

Coffee finally reached the Americas during the 18th century. Coffee houses and coffee products started to sprout, although tea remained America's favorite drink, until 1773, when King George III imposed a heavy tax on tea, and people revolted. This revolt, also known as the Boston Tea Party, instituted coffee as a form of political statement and patriotic duty, and shifted American preference toward coffee since.

This love for caffeine in the form of coffee is best stated by Thomas Jefferson, the 3rd President of the United States of America, when he called coffee *"the favorite drink of the civilized world."*

Industrialization made coffee more accessible and affordable to the masses in the form of instant coffee, also known as freeze-dried coffee. Instant coffee also became the go-to drink of soldiers during the World War. After the war and during years of economic depression, instant coffee became handy. Coffee connoisseurs would usually scoff down at this watered-down version of their freshly-brewed cup of coffee, but this format remains popular even up to today, as evident in the proliferation of many brands and variants of instant coffee, whether pure soluble, ready mix or mixed with sugar and creamer, or in ready-to-drink bottles and cans.

It is quite fascinating how coffee has evolved throughout history. Despite the coffee milestones, from being eaten raw to being boiled to being fermented to finally being roasted, coffee has remained a functional beverage, a legally addicting stimulant that everyone can enjoy, from monks to businessmen to soldiers to students.

Nowadays, it has not lost popularity whatsoever, coffee is widely-available in various forms and preparations. Go to the grocery and supermarket, or perhaps do a pantry check of the houses of your neighbors, and most likely,

you will find coffee beans and/or instant coffee. Walk
down the street in your town or city, near where you
study or work, or where you reside, and most likely, there
will be a coffee shop, whether a locally-owned one-man
store, or a branch of a national or global coffee store
chain.

Most believe 3 waves have been formed in coffee.
The first wave is when coffee became everywhere, it
describes the movement into total mainstream society
around the world in the last few hundred years. The 2nd
wave represents the move to gourmet coffee in the last
few decades. This wave started to educate people on more
artisan types of coffee but aimed at mainstream appeal
with branded quality coffee. Finally, the 3rd wave is the
most recent which is about high quality coffee and coffee
as a science. It's what the 2nd wave aimed at but the 3rd
wave is for more specialty coffee and considers every
aspect of the drink, brew and plant. The transition into a
new era of coffee and the breakdown of every aspect of
the drink comes with complications. This complication is
why I think people need as much information about
coffee as possible.

One of the most iconic 2nd wave coffee shop brands in the
world, Starbucks, opened its first store in Seattle's Pike
Place Market in 1971. Since then, it has opened many
branches all over America. Starbucks arguably spurred
the popularization of a new kind of gourmet coffee, not
just in America, but all over the globe. Starbucks is
currently competing with other popular coffee shop
brands, globally and locally. In fact, if one goes to another
country, whether a developed nation or a developing
country, it is not surprising if there is a global coffee

brand competing with a strong local coffee brand which has grown in popularity. It has started a trend in everyday people getting into gourmet coffee. Starbucks brought high end coffee into mass market heading the 2nd wave movement.

Other popular 2nd wave brands of coffee shops found around the world includes Gloria Jean's Coffees, Seattle's Best Coffee, The Coffee Bean & Tea Leaf (CBTL), and Caribou Coffee. Donut shops are also known for their coffee, such as Dunkin' Donuts, Krispy Kreme, and Tim Hortons. Even fast food restaurant McDonald's boasts of a brand extension, McCafé, featuring specialty coffee. Other famous coffee shops all over the world include UCC (Japan), Ya Kun Kaya Toast (Singapore), Highlands Coffee (Vietnam), Indian Coffee House (India), Oldtown White Coffee (Malaysia), Figaro (Philippines), Paris Croissant (South Korea), Dôme (Australia), The Coffee Club (New Zealand), Costa Coffee (UK), and Caffè Pascucci (Italy). Most of these brands do not just operate locally, but also have presence in other countries. These brands operate in what is considered the 2nd wave.

Some of these brands also offer their own line of retail coffee, from Starbucks Via and bottled frappuccinos to UCC canned coffees. All these amp up the coffee game by encouraging better formulation and more premium coffee line from instant and ready-to-drink coffee brands such as Maxwell House, Folgers, and Nescafe.

Indeed, coffee has become a dynamic and vibrant industry, offering consumers various forms and preparations of the beverage. With such vast coffee options, it appeals to varying palettes and preferences. With the many options available now, one is sure to find at least one kind of coffee that suits one's liking. With its many variations, one can explore and taste the world through coffee. And perhaps, like the Kaldi the herder dancing with his goats, coffee drinkers would dance with energy and joy, exclaiming: "What a time to be alive, with all these coffee and jive!"

With its long history, you can bet the world is likely to have developed a few of its routines around coffee.

The Cultural Role Of Coffee

The cultural role of coffee spreads way beyond just a simple beverage. The society has adopted coffee in so many interesting ways:

Cafés or coffee shops

Coffee shops/coffeehouses are literally all over the place these days. They were initially set up to serve coffee or a variety of other hot drinks. They were—and still are—locations where people meet up or individually go to read, write, talk, or just pass time. Who hasn't uttered the words- "Coffee date?".

Most coffee shops nowadays, especially American coffee chains, function as a "third home" of customers where they can use Wi-Fi, whether for free or with minimal fee, as well as charge their laptops and gadgets, while they catch up with friends or do some work. Some stay in coffee shops for hours, studying solo or in groups, or meeting with colleagues and clients. Coffee shops serve as modern libraries and meeting hubs. Coffee shops have flourished with technology and adapted accordingly to meet demands.

Coffee culture in movies, comics and television is quite evident. Popular TV shows such as *NCIS* and many more, the actors constantly hold espressos or some characters pass out take-out cups of coffee to the others. In fact, the spread of coffee culture in Ireland is largely accredited to the shows *Friends* and *Frasier* according to Philip Nolan, a *Daily Mail* writer. Both shows have the characters always sipping coffee—and not booze.

As a stimulant with strong caffeine content, coffee accelerates the heart beat and stimulates blood flow. It is no wonder that people also consider it an aphrodisiac, apart from being a social drink. These explain coffee's presence in the popular culture of romance. Perhaps you would know or have heard of the 1970s-comedy book that turned into movie, the title of which has become a catchphrase over the years: *Coffee, Tea, or Me?*

The classic coffee breaks

A coffee break is a social gathering done on routine by employees in an industry or business to get a snack and take a breather. The break is said to have originated in Stoughton, Wisconsin in the 19th century where immigrant men agreed to work only if they could go home every morning and afternoon for some coffee—the city celebrates the Stoughton Coffee Break Festival.

"Science may never come up with a better office communication system than the coffee break." - Earl Wilson

A-Z List of How To Make Coffee

After exploring the history and significance of coffee, let us now explore the basics of coffee, from the coffee beans, coffee equipment, to the numerous coffee preparations that span from A to Z. Read on, maybe with a cup of your favorite coffee beverage in hand.

The Essence of Coffee: Coffee Beans

There are generally four types of coffee beans: Arabica, Robusta, other types, and blended types.

Arabica and Robusta are the most common species of coffee beans cultivated and used. Arabica is considered having higher quality than Robusta in terms of origin and taste profile.

Arabica is grown in high altitude, usually in shaded areas of mountains above 600 meters. By contrast, Robusta, also known as *Coffea canephora*, is usually grown in low altitude, making it easier to cultivate and harvest. Robusta beans are also more resistant to diseases and insects, and less vulnerable to changes in weather, which is becoming the norm amid global warming. Since Arabica beans require more care, they are pricier than Robusta.

Arabica is predominantly cultivated in Latin America

and some parts of Africa, specifically Brazil, Colombia, Ethiopia, Peru, Honduras, and Mexico. Meanwhile, Robusta is notably grown in the Eastern Hemisphere, notably in Africa and Asia such as Vietnam, Indonesia, and India. It is also cultivated in some Latin American countries such as Brazil.

Though Robusta is widely-available, Arabica still accounts for roughly three-fourth of coffee production. Indeed, there is clamor for the taste of good quality Arabica coffee. This is not to say that all Arabica beans are created equal, as there are some inferior Arabica coffee beans that are not deemed suitable as base beans of specialty coffee. All other factors being equal though, if we put the best Arabica coffee and the best Robusta coffee side by side in their simplest brewed state, most coffee fans would probably prefer the taste of the Arabica.

Arabica has sweet and acidic taste with well-balanced flavor, and may have pleasantly fruity, floral, chocolatey, caramelly, and nutty notes, depending on its area of origin. On the other hand, Robusta has more bitter taste with flat and grainy flavor, with tinges of taste of burnt peanut, burnt wood, or burnt rubber. Arabica has higher acidity and less caffeine. By contrast, Robusta has roughly twice more caffeine, making it taste stronger and harsher. Good quality Robusta is often used as the base of instant coffee.

Apart from origin and taste, the two types also differ in terms of look and aroma. Arabica beans are oval, Robusta more circular. An Arabica bean has more pronounced center crease. Robusta beans tend to be paler.

Before roasting, Arabica beans smell sweet like

blueberries, while Robusta beans smell quite nutty. During brewing, Robusta beans tend to be more aromatic, having more robust aroma, hence its name. Robusta also yields more crema, making it ideal filler especially when making espresso. Specialty coffee shops and coffee manufacturers often blend Arabica and Robusta beans to get the best of both worlds: the full-bodied flavor and high acidity of Arabica plus the aroma, crema, high caffeine content, and cheap price of Robusta.

Aside from Arabica and Robusta, there are other minor species of coffee beans cultivated around the globe, such as Liberica or Barako (Philippines) and the newly-discovered caffeine-free Charrieriana (Cameroon, Central Africa). There are also varieties of Arabica and Robusta. For instance, Kopi Luwak (Indonesia, Vietnam) and Kapeng Alamid (Philippines) are Robusta beans eaten, digested, and secreted by the mammal palm civet or toddy cat. The digestive process of the civet gives the coffee beans a unique flavor. Civet coffee is known to be very expensive and controversial due to animal welfare issues.

There are many species, variants, and blends of coffee beans available in the market. You can buy beans from your favorite coffee shop, brew these beans at home, prepare them with your preferred additions and toppings, and enjoy your usual coffee shop drink for the fraction of the price! You can also try the beans sold in groceries, public markets, or specialty stores.

With the many types and blends out there, you are sure to find something that suits your taste profile. Just choose beans wisely and mindfully. Even coffee brands are going for more sustainable, responsibly-sourced, environment-friendly, socially-conscious, and fair-trade coffee bean options.

The Science and Art of Coffee: Tips and Guidelines on Coffee-Making

Each sip of coffee makes you a part of the long history of coffee. Knowing how the beans end up into that rich cup of coffee goodness would also enable you to have a deeper appreciation of its aroma, flavor, sensation, and benefits beyond taste. Let us travel the route of coffee: from bean to cup.

Roasting Coffee

We discussed in the earlier section the various types of beans. It doesn't end there. Coffee beans need roasting. During the early years of coffee, the beans were eaten raw, boiled, or made into energy snacks. We should thank the Arabs for discovering the roasting method in the 13th century.

Before roasting, coffee beans are colored green. During the roasting procedure, then turn from light brown to dark brown to almost black in color. At 400°F, the beans start to roast and their chemistry starts to change. As the temperature reaches 450°F to 500°F, the beans lose their acidity and caffeine and start to acquire more body and heavier texture. As it becomes darker and darker in color nearing black, the natural oils come to the surface. Beyond this point or at higher heat levels, the beans burn, dry, and lose taste, flavor, and oil altogether.

The good thing is that you need not do this roasting process, as there are trusted, specialized, and highly-skilled roastmasters who do this for coffee fans. You can try roasting coffee at home, but it requires exact science to roast the beans to perfection, and you need to study this well, perhaps read extensively or train under a roastmaster, otherwise there is that risk of burning and wasting good quality beans.

When buying roasted coffee, you should be familiar with roast lexicon. Terminologies vary per country, but there are typically 3 types or levels of roasts.

Light Roast. This is also known as mild, blond, or American roast. Light in color, it has mild and sweet flavor.

Medium Roast. Also known as regular, breakfast, or morning roast, it has fuller body and less acidity.

Dark Roast. Dark brown to almost black in color, these roasted beans are oily and rich in flavor. Usual types include French roast and Espresso roast. Dark Espresso roast is nearly black, and given its longer roasting time, has less caffeine versus other roasts.

Aside from roasts, there are also other types of coffee beans: decaffeinated and flavored. Let us briefly look at how they are manufactured.

Decaffeinated Coffee or Decaf. Caffeine naturally occurs in coffee, except for the newly-discovered caffeine-free specie Charrieriana. Decaffeination is the process of taking out the caffeine in coffee. Coffee beans are decaffeinated before roasting. There are many methods of decaffeination, but in general, water is used to wash away caffeine, and to speed up the process, chemicals such as methylene chloride and activated charcoal are used. The trick is to retain its natural flavor and chemicals, so that coffee drinkers would still enjoy coffee sans caffeine kick. Note though that decaf is not entirely free of caffeine, just 97% caffeine-free.

Flavored Coffee. Some people like to flavor their coffee with nuts, fruits, spices, and herbs. Some do this during or after brewing. Another option is to flavor the beans themselves. This is usually done during roasting. As beans cool down, flavoring can be added, such as hazelnut, chocolate, cinnamon, amaretto, butterscotch, caramel, mint, and raspberry, among others. Flavored coffee has been notorious in the past for using flavors to mask inferior coffee beans. Nowadays, more subtle and sophistical flavored coffee beans are available, using high quality beans and flavoring.

As you explore the different types and roasts of beans, feel free to mix and match to create your own blend. Perhaps you would find decaffeinated medium roast hazelnut-infused Arabica as a nice way to cap the day and lull you to sleep at night, while having 50% light roast and 50% dark roast as your go-to drink in the morning.

Grinding Coffee

Coffee beans reach their peak flavor 4 to 7 days after roasting, but you can store roasted beans for months. It is best to buy whole bean coffee, as ground coffee tends to lose flavor and aroma faster. Hence, coffee enthusiasts often have coffee grinder at home so that they brew freshly-ground coffee every time. If you prefer ground coffee, make sure that you consume it within 7 days. Whichever the case, it is still wise to learn about coffee grinds, as there are specific grind types suited for particular coffee preparations. There are 4 types of coffee grinds.

Coarse Grind. Larger or coarser pieces of coffee are suitable for preparations that require longer water steeping such as percolator and cold brew.

Medium Grind. This grind is suitable for water dripping preparations such as filter method and electric drip coffeemakers with flat-bottomed filter baskets.

Fine Grind. This is often used for flip drips and manual filters, and can also be used for electric drip coffeemakers with cone-shaped filter baskets or paper cone filters such as Krups and Melitta.

Extra-Fine Grind. This powder-fine coffee grind is perfect for espresso that requires high pressured water to run through tightly-packed coffee grinds. It is also used in Turkish coffee.

These are just the general terms to describe how coarse or how fine coffee beans can be. Coffee roasters often have grinding machines specific to the coffee preparation you have in mind. Don't be surprised and baffled if they ask you if the coffee grind you need is for French press, cone drip, flat-bottomed drip, moka pot, percolator, or espresso machine. To avoid being clueless, read the next section on different types and equipment of coffee brewing.

Do not be limited by the grind-preparation matching. Feel free to use fine or extra-fine grinds for other methods such as the regular electric coffeemaker, if you don't mind coffee sediments.

Brewing Coffee

There are several options for brewing coffee, and each one yields a unique cup. Here are 6 common coffee-brewing equipment.

Drip Coffee. It can be electric or manual, with or without filter, and the filter can be cone or basket. Perhaps the most common equipment in households is the electric drip coffee filter requiring either cone or basket paper filter for easier cleaning. The machine heats the water, brews the coffee by running water through the beans, and dripping the coffee-infused liquid into a carafe, which is kept warm by a heated plate.

This method is convenient as you just need to load the beans and water, turn the machine on, do something else, and come back to that whiff of freshly-brewed coffee, ready to be poured and enjoyed in a cup or mug. It's joyous to wake up to the smell of coffee in the morning prepared by a housemate or family member!

Drip brewing began with the brewing pot called biggin, way back 1780 in France. This pot has two levels. Ground coffee was placed in the upper compartment, into which hot water was poured. The water then drains or drips to the bottom compartment, with a cloth filtering the sediments. The drawback of this method was that the taste of the cloth tends to transfer to the taste of the coffee. During those days, people used cotton or old pieces of clothing, even old socks, as coffee filters. Thankfully, we have more modern equipment nowadays.

The first automatic/electric drip coffeemaker was launched by Bunn Corporation in 1963. This was used commercially, for restaurants and coffee shops. It was almost a decade later that coffeemaker became available to household, thanks to Vincent Marotta who released the first home-use automatic drip coffeemaker in 1972. It was aptly named Mr. Coffee.

Aside from electric coffee drip machines, manual dripping equipment are also available, from the simple single-serve pour-overs such as Vietnamese phin filter and German brand Melitta, to the fancy Neapolitan flip drips.

Coffee Press. Also, known as cafetiere or plunger pot, this entails placing medium-ground coffee in the glass or plastic carafe, pouring hot water over the coffee, letting it steep for at least 5 minutes, then pressing the plunger to force the grounds to the bottom of the pot, separating it from the liquid coffee drink.

Espresso Machine. This is often seen in coffee shops and in houses of coffee connoisseurs. There are various brands available in the market. For instance, Starbucks uses Mastrena. Espresso machines work by forcing a stream of water to run through tightly-packed finely-ground espresso beans.

Stove-Top Espresso Pot. This is a non-electric fancy-looking espresso-maker. It is also known as moka espresso pot, the most popular brand of which is Bialetti. This equipment works by putting cold water in the bottom cylinder of the pot, putting the basket on top of this pot and putting coffee beans in the basket, screwing the pot with the top cylinder, putting it on the stove, and heating it. The machine hisses, signaling that the water is forced up to the grounds and to the upper carafe. Take it out of the heat once the hissing starts to get irregular, usually just a few seconds after the hissing starts. There are also espresso pots that can be used on electric and induction stoves. Think of espresso pots as upside-down versions of espresso machines.

Stove-Top Coffee Pot. This is a special pot to brew coffee. An example is Ibrik, small long-handled copper or brass pot used to prepare and serve Turkish coffee.

Percolator. This machine dates back to the 1940s and 1950s. It is an electric pot that heats the water, forces it up through a tube in the center, and circulates the water over the bed of coarsely-ground coffee. It is rarely used nowadays, as over-exposure to water results to over-extraction which diminishes the flavor and freshness of coffee.

Coffee Pod or Capsule Brewing Machine. This brewing system entered the coffee arena in the early 21st century. The machine processes specially-manufactured pods or capsules of coffee. You load a pod into a machine, and the machine brews it to produce a single-serve cup of coffee. Popular brands include Keurig K-Cups and Nescafé Dolce Gusto. Coffee shops also offer coffee pod machines, such as Starbucks and CBTL. They offer different variants and flavors of coffee.

In 2010 though, this method, especially K-Cups, was widely criticized due to environmental concerns regarding the disposal and non-biodegradable quality of the pods. This encouraged various brands to market biodegradable, reusable, or recyclable pods.

Storing Coffee

Buy coffee as fresh as possible, and store it properly to retain its freshness. You can store unroasted coffee beans for up to 6 months, as long as you keep it away from dampness, heat, and strong odors. If you would rather buy roasted beans as other people do, follow the storage guideline as follows.

Unopened or sealed whole beans can last for 6 to 9 months in the pantry, and 2 to 3 years in the freezer. However, it is best to consume it within its peak freshness, which is 4 to 7 days upon roasting.

Meanwhile, unopened or sealed ground coffee lasts for 3 to 5 months in the pantry, and 1 to 2 years in the freezer. However, it is best to consume ground coffee within 7 days upon opening the sealed pack. It is not advisable to keep coffee in the refrigerator or freezer and take it out on a daily basis as this causes condensation and moisture is bad for coffee.

In fact, do not store coffee at all in the refrigerator and freezer unless you really need to. To get the maximum flavor of coffee, buy newly-roasted whole bean coffee frequently in small quantities just enough for 7 days, store it in airtight glass container at room temperature, and grind the beans just before brewing. Adjust and compromise based on your lifestyle, preferences, and access to beans and machines.

Cleaning and Recycling

On Cloth Filter: Wash it after every use by running and rinsing it under cold tap clean water. Do not use soap as the taste of soap may transfer to the coffee the next time you use it. Hang it to dry to prevent mildew. Replace your cloth filters every couple of months.

On Used Ground Coffee: You can use this as fertilizer, odor absorber, face mask, face rub, or dry it fully and use it to stuff pincushions.

On Calibrating Equipment: Clean and calibrate your coffee equipment every now and then, following the manufacturer's instructions. For regular electric drip coffeemaker, it is usually cleaned every couple of months. To clean and calibrate, fill its water chamber with vinegar solution: equal parts white vinegar and water. Brew until half the chamber is empty, then turn the machine off. Let it sit for 30 minutes. After which, finish brewing. Throw away the vinegar solution in the carafe. Brew water in 1 to 3 cycles until the vinegar smell comes off.

Other equipment requires specific care and calibration. It is important to do this properly and regularly to ensure that your equipment would run well and last long.

Coffee Preparations and Styles

The most basic way to take coffee is to take it black—no sugar, cream or milk—just plain old coffee in water. As much as black coffee is still tasty this way, there are so many other exciting ways to make coffee—keeping the different types of coffee brands out of mind. They say that once you go black, you never go back. But this shouldn't stop you from exploring other types and variations of coffee.

The most common additions to coffee are milk, cream, spices, and butter, but there are many other ingredients depending on where and who makes the drink.

Coffee is adopted all over the world so each region, country, or continent has their own different way of making coffee. There are so many ways to make coffee such that you would need a couple of months to taste a new variation of coffee daily.

And with that said, you might want to prepare your throat as you read and prepare all the coffee drinks that you can think of and so much more. The drinks will be arranged in alphabetical order so you can feel free to jump to any drink that catches your fancy. Let's begin!

A

Affogato

This coffee based drink started in Italy where the bitterness of the espresso would be complemented by the ice cream. It can be just a drink or a dessert.

Affogato (meaning 'drowned' in Italian) is basically a scoop of ice cream with an espresso. Most of the time, it takes the form of an ice cream that is topped with a shot of hot espresso or a scoop of vanilla gelato with a shot of hot espresso. An Affogato could also include a shot of Amaretto or any of your favorite liqueurs.

Note

Espresso is the name given to a bittersweet highly concentrated coffee—or the brewing method to get the espresso. Finely ground coffee is tamped with about 30 pounds of pressure pre-infused with almost boiling water (to get the coffee wet). After that, it is extracted within 30 seconds, approximately, under minimal 9 bar pump pressure. The result is an exquisite potion with a syrupy texture and about 4mm thick crema.

*Crema is a thin layer of foam formed at the top of a cup of coffee.

An espresso shot size is defined as 1 fluid ounce shot for a single shot. Double would be 2 fluid ounces, triple would be 3 and so on. Each shot contains an equal amount of ground coffee. For instance, a single shot has 7 grams, double 14 grams and triple 21 grams.

How to make it

Ingredients

Espresso/strong brewed coffee

Ice cream (vanilla/chocolate/coffee)

Instructions

Add 2 small scoops of vanilla, coffee or chocolate ice cream into a coffee cup and pour in 3 tablespoons of strong brewed coffee or 1 shot of espresso. You can top it with chopped hazelnuts or shaved dark chocolate.

Antoccino

Despite its name, it doesn't have any link to Italy or meaning in Italian. This is a single espresso shot combined with steamed milk in the ratio of 1:1 and is served in an espresso cup.

How to make it

Ingredients

1 ounce of espresso

1 ounce of steamed milk

Instructions

Brew espresso and add it to an espresso cup. Steam the whole milk and pour it on top of the espresso.

Americano

This is a famous coffee drink sold globally although not so popular in 'the land of espresso'—Italy. The drink is designed to be similar to coffee that is brewed in a drip filter. It is made by combining hot steaming water (about 4 to 5 ounces) with a single or double shot of espresso (readymade espresso) in a 2 demitasse cup.

*Demitasse: it is a measurement of coffee translating to half a cup (4 ounces).

How to make it

Ingredients

2/3 Hot water

1/3 Espresso

Instructions

Have a coffee mug or a latte mug ready. Pull a 3-ounce espresso shot in a different glass (you can pull more if you like it stronger). Pour more than 3 ounces of hot water to the mug you will be drinking from and add in the espresso shot. There goes your Americano!

B

Babycino

This is a cappuccino-like drink served in affluent cafés meant for children. Don't worry: no espresso coffee essence is added to Babycino. The drink consists of warm milk added to a small cup then topped with some milk froth with chocolate powder on top.

S0 next time you go to a coffee shop with your child and feel guilty about it, just buy him/her a cup of Babycino.

Baltimore

This contains equal parts decaffeinated and caffeinated coffee. It is also called Half-Caf.

Bicerin

This is a traditional warm coffee brew made of espresso, whole milk and drinking chocolate carefully layered in a small round glass. Bicerin is actually a Piedmontese name meaning small glass. It originated from Turin, Italy.

How to make it

Ingredients

A thick-sided glass (stemmed) with a volume equal to 1 cup per person

Espresso Coffee- sweetened to taste

Hot milk whipped to a creamy froth

Hot Chocolate (thick and creamy)

Instructions

Fill your glass ¼ full with espresso then add in the hot chocolate then the hot frothy milk 1/4 full too to make the glass about three quarters full. Ensure that you don't stir and you will get a thick dark layer with a creamy layer on top.

Black Coffee

This is the good old filter coffee with absolutely no additions. It is served just after brewing, which makes it perfect to savor the rich pure flavor of coffee. You can also have black coffee with milk and/or sugar.

Just add some cream or milk if you love that creamy taste and artificial sweetener or sugar if you have a sweet tooth.

Black Tie

This is a coffee-tea concoction from Thailand. This traditional Thai iced tea-coffee drink is made by mixing chilled black tea, spices, condensed milk or cream, and double shot espresso, resulting to a spicy-sweet drink. Usual spices added are: orange blossom water, star anise, and crushed tamarind. It is called a Red Tie if it only has one shot of espresso.

Coffee houses offer their own interpretations and variations of the drink. For example, American coffee shop Peet's Coffee & Tea uses cold brew as coffee base, chicory syrup as additional flavor, and half and half as for that layer of cream float.

Borgia

This is mocha with orange rind or sometimes orange flavor. It is usually served with whipped cream then topped with cinnamon.

Botz

This is a simple and easy way of drinking coffee adopted in Israel. Botz means 'mud'.

How to make it

You simply add finely ground coffee to a cup. Pour in boiling water into the cup. Let it stand for a couple of minutes to settle and cool.

The coffee is then drunk leaving the grounds in the cup.

Breve

This is a milk based espresso where instead of using

milk, half and half is used. Café breve is foamier than a latte.

*Half and half is simply a mixture of milk and cream.

How to make it

Ingredients

Espresso

Steamed half and half

Instructions

Add the half and half in a microwave safe measuring cup (1 cup). Microwave while uncovered for a minute on the high setting until small bubbles are visible all around the cup.

Whisk using a metal whisk and remove the foam to a measuring cup and keep on whisking until you get 1/3 cup of foam. Set aside.

Pour the espresso into a cup and the remaining half and half just after. Spoon the foam to the top and serve right away.

Bulletproof Coffee

This was developed and popularized by David Asprey after tasting yak-butter tea in Tibet. His recipe starts with a cup of freshly-brewed Bulletproof Coffee, upgraded coffee beans sold by Bulletproof Nutrition. The following ingredients are then added to this 8-oz. brewed coffee: 1 tbsp. grass-fed unsalted butter or ghee and 1 tsp of Brain Octane Oil, extracted from coconut oil. Mix all these in a blender for 20 to 30 seconds until the concoction turns frothy.

The original Bulletproof Coffee recipe calls for ingredients sold by Asprey's company. The product claims to boost cognitive performance, spur weight loss, and make one more energetic. The product appeals to various people such as athletes and entrepreneurs.

While Bulletproof Coffee is branded and trademarked, you can buy it from some coffee shops who have their own version of bulletproof coffee method, and you can even make it at home by just replacing the branded ingredients with the ones you have in your pantry.

Just add a pat of unsalted butter in your coffee and mix it well. You can even use salted butter. Or you can stir in a teaspoon of extra virgin coconut oil in the coffee, with or without butter.

Bulletproof coffee is a matter of taste: you either like it or you don't. Try it once and check where you fall in the spectrum.

Buna (Ethiopian Coffee)

This is not just a cup or a method of coffee-making, but rather a coffee ceremony in Ethiopia.

It is usually officiated by the woman of an Ethiopian

COFFEE: THE LITTLE EVERYTHING GUIDE

household. To participate in this ceremony or to be offered a place in this ceremony is considered an honor.

The ceremony starts by roasting the green coffee beans. This is done in a pan, over an open flame. The freshly-roasted coffee is then grinded using the traditional wooden mortar and pestle. After which, the newly-ground coffee beans are then boiled in a special vessel called jebena, then strained through a sieve several times.

The hose pours coffee for all guests. Brewing and serving happens thrice: first cup is called *awel* or *abol*, the second cup is *tona* or *kale'i*, and the last cup is called *baraka* which means "to be blessed". Usual add-ons to the cups of coffee are sugar, salt, and traditional butter (niter kibbeh). Milk is not usually added.

Traditional incense is also typically burned during the ceremony. Snacks are also served such as popcorn, peanuts, himbasha or celebration bread, and kolo or grain mix.

C

Cà Phê Đá (Cafe Da)

This is a traditional Vietnamese coffee, made using dark roast coffee beans brewed using a small metal Vietnamese drip filter also called phin filter.

To use the phin filter, put in on top of a regular cup. Take out the cover and the damper. Put 1 tablespoon of ground coffee. Put back the damper, press it, and turn slightly to tamp. Pour a small amount of water, and let it rest for 30 seconds to allow the coffee to bloom. After 30 seconds, fill the filter all the way with water, then put the lid/cover on to keep the heat in.

Since the ground coffee beans are pressed and tamped with the damper, dripping occurs slowly, resulting to a strong cup of coffee. You can also immerse the cup in a larger cup or bowl with hot water to keep it hot/warm longer.

It becomes *cà phê sữa nóng* or hot milk coffee when it is dripped into a cup containing sweetened condensed milk. When the milk coffee is poured over ice, it is then called *cà phê sữa đá* or iced milk coffee.

Cà Phê Trứng (Vietnamese Egg Coffee)

This drink literally contains egg. To make this, start by making cà phê đá using phin filter. Or you can just use strongly-brewed coffee, or espresso. Put the serving cup in a larger cup or bowl filled with hot water. This immersion will slightly cook the egg cream later on. Fill half of the serving cup with strong coffee, then pour in egg cream, then pour the remaining coffee in. Robusta beans are perfect for this type of preparation as its bitterness is contrasted and balanced by the thick and creamy egg cream. You can also use Arabica or mixed blend.

To make egg cream, beat two fresh egg yolks with 1 tablespoon sugar, 3 tablespoons condensed milk, a tablespoon of vanilla, and a tablespoon of the coffee liquid. You can whisk manually or use an electric mixer.

The result is a strong and creamy drink, earning its label as "liquid tiramisu". This has been a staple in Hanoi, Vietnam since the 1950s. It also started to gain popularity in Ho Chi Minh City coffee shops in the 21st century.

Café au lait

This is a French coffee drink which is the same as 'café con leche 'in Spain, 'Milchkaffee' in Germany, 'café latte' in Italy, 'café com leite' in Portugal, 'kawa biala' in Poland, 'koffie verkeerd' in Netherlands and 'Grosser Brauner' in Austria, which simply means coffee with milk. The most used name in Europe is café au lait.

The drink consists of bold or strong coffee (espresso is used sometimes) mixed with steamed or scalded milk in an approximate ratio of 1:1.

How to make it

Ingredients

1 part steamed milk

1 part hot coffee

Instructions

Add milk to saucepan and heat over medium low heat as you whisk until the milk turns a bit foamy and steams. Add the milk to a large coffee cup or a café au lait bowl. Add coffee to fill the cup or bowl. Stir.

Café Bombon

This drink (bombon which means confection in Spanish) was first made popular in Valencia in Spain then eventually spread to the whole country. From there, it moved all around notably to Europe and Asia- although it was tweaked a little to suit European tastes.

The drink has several variations. For instance, the Asian version of a bombon uses unsweetened condensed milk and ground coffee at the same ratio while the European version uses sweet condensed milk and espresso at the same ratio.

For serving, a café bombon is served in a glass for the visual effect where the condensed milk is added to the coffee slowly to sink beneath the coffee and create 2 lines of different colors- but the layers are normally mixed together just before drinking. In some places, an espresso is served separately with a sachet of condensed milk so that the customer can make their own bombon.

How to make it

Ingredients

½ espresso

½ condensed milk (sweetened)

Instructions

Add the espresso shots into a clear glass. Add the condensed milk carefully to fill the glass with espresso making sure not to ruin the layering effect. You can also do this in reverse if desired- condensed milk first then espresso.

Café de Olla

This is a traditional Mexican coffee preparation. It literally means pot coffee, because it is prepared in earthen clay pots, usually made by artisan potters. The coffee is typically flavored with cinnamon and piloncillo or panela, which are blocks or cubes of Mexican sugar. The earthen clay pot also gives a distinct flavor to the drink. It is a usual drink in the cold and rural areas.

Café Miel

This drink contains one shot of espresso with steamed

milk, cinnamon, and honey. Miel means honey in French.

Caffè Corretto

This is an Italian drink that is made of a shot of liquor (normally grappa and sometimes brandy or sambuca) and a shot of espresso. Out of Italy, it is referred to as 'espresso corretto'. If you are to order it, name it as 'un caffe corretto alla grappa/sambuca/cognac' or the liquor that you desire.

Carajillo, kaffekask and karsk are a similar drink in Spain, Sweden and Norway respectively.

How to make it

Ingredients

Freshly ground espresso

1 shot of grappa

Sugar

Instructions

Brew a shot of espresso and add it to your espresso cup. Add in the shot of grappa and add in sugar to taste. This is great to enjoy after a meal or just when you want it!

Caffè Crema

This is a long espresso initially served in Austria, Southern Switzerland and the northern Italy. The best way to make it is to make it chilled.

Note:

Long espresso- it is a coffee drink made by an espresso machine to brew an Italian style coffee. It is a single or double shot with added water making it a larger coffee. It is also known as 'lungo'.

How to make it

Ingredients

1 cup chilled strong coffee/ espresso

2 cups crushed ice

3 tablespoons confectioners' sugar

1/2 cup half-and-half

Instructions

Add all ingredients to a blender and combine until creamy. Add to tall glasses and drink right away.

*Have your coffee brewed double strength to compensate for possible dilution from ice.

Caffè Freddo

This is any chilled/iced coffee that is sweetened and

served in a tall glass.

This is quite similar with Vietnamese cà phê sữa đá or iced milk coffee, and the Spanish beverages Café del Tiempo (Summer Weather Coffee) and Café con Hielo (Coffee with Ice).

Caffè Macchiato

This is an espresso based drink that comprises of mostly coffee and a small addition of milk. In Italian, it means marked coffee which means that the espresso is 'marked' with a few drops of frothed milk and drank from a demitasse cup.

Compared to other drinks based on espresso, caffe macchiato is way closer to straight espresso as it contains literally only a few drops of milk.

How to make it

Ingredients

¼ cup milk

½ cup espresso

Instructions

Whip the milk using a frother until foamy. Divide the espresso equally between the espresso cups and spoon the formed milk foam on top to taste.

There are also variations. Single shot espresso is called short macchiato, while double shot is called long macchiato. *Short* and *long* simply refer to the quantity of liquid.

Caffé Mélange

This is a creamy coffee based drink is especially popular in Netherlands, Austria and Switzerland. It is simply black coffee mixed (mélange in French) with whipped cream or covered on top with whipped cream. Cocoa or chocolate powder can also be added as a variation. It also goes by the names Wiener Mélange, Wiener, or Viennese melange.

How to make it

Ingredients

100 ml coffee

1 teaspoon grated chocolate or cocoa powder

1 tablespoon whipped cream

Instructions

Prepare coffee using 100ml of water and top the coffee with whipped cream. Use a little grated chocolate or a dust of cocoa to garnish. You can serve with some sugar.

Coffee Milk

Coffee milk is similar to chocolate milk although coffee syrup is used instead of chocolate syrup. This is Rhode Island's official state drink.

It was created by a creative diner operator who sweetened some left-over coffee grounds with sugar and milk which formed an extract that was molasses like- this is what the coffee syrup is.

How to make it

Ingredients

1 cup coffee syrup (e.g. Eclipse)

2 quarts of cold 2% or whole milk

Instructions

Take a large pitcher and add in coffee syrup and milk. Mix until well blended and drink up.

Cappuccino

This is an espresso based drink basically made from milk and espresso- more precisely, 1/3 of espresso, 1/3 of milk foam and 1/3 of heated milk served in a 6-8 ounce cup.

The original Italian cappuccino consists of 1 shot of espresso (about 1.26 ounces) topped with a small amount of froth and milk. Usually, a cappuccino is without any garnishes and flavorings except a bit of unsweetened chocolate powder.

How to make it

Ingredients

Espresso

Frothed milk

Milk foam

Instructions

Add a shot of espresso to a large cup and add in an equal amount of frothed milk. Top with some foam and enjoy.

If you want to perform some latte art, use a clear cup and break a leg.

There are also variations of cappuccino. Cappuccino scuro, also called dry or dark cappuccino, contains less milk than usual. It is something between a cappuccino and a macchiato. Meanwhile, cappuccino chiaro, also known as wet or light cappuccino, has more milk than usual.

For a stronger version, two shots of espresso can be used, and this is called cappuccino con doppio caffe. When cappuccino is served over ice, it is called cappuccino freddo, literally meaning iced Cappuccino. Lastly, when skim or nonfat milk is used, it is dubbed as skinny cappuccino.

Chai Latte

Just because it has latte in its name doesn't mean it has coffee! Latte came from the Latin word *lactis* which means milk. It is popularly used as caffe latte which means milk coffee, eventually latte by itself took on the connotation as being a coffee drink.

But chai latte does not contain coffee, though it contains caffeine in another form—tea. It literally means *milk tea*.

To make chai latte, you can use tea powder, tea bags, or dried tea leaves. After brewing the tea, add any type of milk as desired. Sweeteners can also be added, whether white or refined sugar, brown sugar, stevia, artificial sweeteners, coco sugar, honey, etc. You can also add other spices and flavorings such as cinnamon, all-spice, nutmeg, hazelnut, and caramel, among others.

Carajillo

This drink of Spain origin is made by combining brandy or rum with coffee. The troops of Spain used to combine rum with coffee to give them courage to go on battle.

How to make it

There are several ways to make Carajillo—like from spirit mixed with black coffee to heating the spirit with cinnamon, lemon and sugar and finally adding coffee.

Caffe corretto is an Italian drink similar to this.

Cortado

Cortado, from the Spanish word 'cortar', which means to cut in the sense of diluting, is an espresso 'cut' with a bit of some warm milk to reduce its acidity. The milk is added after the espresso and the ratio of the coffee to milk is in between 1:1 and 1:2. The steamed milk does not have much foam although most baristas use some micro-foam to create latte art.

The coffee is served in a special glass with a metal wire handle and a metal ring base. There are a few variations of Cortado including bombon/Cortado condensada, which is espresso with condensed milk and leche y leche which is the same as bombon but with cream on top.

This drink is popular in Argentina.

The difference

Sometimes the difference between a caffe macchiato and a cortado beats some people. As explained earlier, a caffe macchiato is an espresso with steamed milk/foam added in the ratio of 1:1 (or less traditionally). It differs from a cortado in that it has more foam as it is a small latte. Besides, the milk of a cortado must be steamed, that's the essence of the drink, and must be served in a 5-7 ounce glass. A cortado is much like a cappuccino that is less foamy than a macchiato.

A similar drink is Piccolo café latte (or simply Piccolo) in Australia. This is a shot of espresso served in a macchiato glass and filled with steamed milk.

How to make it

Ingredients

Steamed milk

Espresso

Instructions

Steam some milk until it is just steamed and not foamy and pour it into a stainless pitcher. Pour espresso to a glass and add in the steamed milk. For a creamier and less bitter flavor, add in more milk.

Café Cubano

Café Cubano also known as Cuban espresso, cafecito, Cuban shot, Cuban coffee or Cuban is an espresso based drink that originated from Cuba. It specifically refers to an espresso sweetened with demerara sugar during the brewing process- although it covers the drinks that use Cuban coffee as their base.

How to make it

There are a number of ways to prepare café Cubano.

The traditional Cuban way of making café Cubano is by adding demerara sugar into the cup or mug where the espresso will drip, which will allow it to mix with the sugar during the brewing process.

Another common method of making Cuban coffee is through adding only a few drops of the espresso to the sugar first and mixing to form a light creamy brown paste. The rest of the espresso is dripped into this paste and mixed which results into a light brown layer of foam (known as espumita) at the top of the coffee. You can either use an espresso machine or a macchinetta (an Italian moka pot).

Note:

Adding sugar during the brewing process results to a different tasting and sweeter coffee as compared to adding sugar at the end because the heat produced during the coffee brewing process hydrolyzes some of the sucrose.

Cafezinho

This coffee preparation is from Brazil. To make cafezinho, add the water and sugar in a pan, and dissolve the sugar well. Bring it to a just below boiling point over medium heat. When it is almost boiling, add finely-ground coffee and stir well. It is crucial not to use boiling water as this will overcook the coffee and make it more bitter. After a few seconds of steeping, pour it slowly through a traditional cloth strainger or a paper filter. It can take quite a while. When done, transfer the liquid to a tiny cup. You may also opt to drip it directly to a small cup such as an espresso cup.

Cold Brew

It is also called as cold water extract or cold press. Cold brew entails seeping coarse-ground coffee beans in water for 12 to 24 hours, whether at room temperature or chilled in the refrigerator. The grounds are strained or filtered out using various methods such as coffee press, paper coffee filter, or metal sieve. There is also equipment specifically made for cold brew, such as Toddy Cold Brew Coffeemaker. There are also methods that require dripping water through coarse coffee grounds for hours, such as DIY bottle method or Kyoto-style slow-drip cold brew.

Because the beans do not come into contact with hot water, cold brew yields coffee that is not as acidic and bitter as hot-brewed coffee. Cold brew concentrate can be used as a replacement for espresso in iced coffee preparations. It is perfect as a hot summer afternoon drink. Some even use it for baking and cooking. There are also available cold brew products in groceries, specialty coffee stores, and coffee shops. You can make it at home too.

When making cold brew at home, use coarse-ground high quality Arabica beans. The ideal ratio is 250 grams ground coffee beans to 2 liters of water, or if you are making a big batch, the ratio would be 1 pound ground coffee beans (roughly 500 grams) to 1 gallon of water (roughly 4 liters). You can add more beans or lessen water if you prefer more concentrated coffee. You can use cold brew equipment or just do it yourself using coffee press, mason jars, or regular jars or bottles you have at home.

Cold brew can keep in the refrigerator for 2 weeks, although its flavor would start to degrade after 7 days. It is best to consume cold brew within a week of extraction. It is wise to take out only the amount that you need every time, as cold brew concentrate mixed with water will only last for 2 to 3 days in the refrigerator.

⍰

D

Doppio

This means double in Italian. It is simply a double shot of espresso. In most coffee shops, they simply list out the shots as single double etc.; they hardly name a double shot as Doppio.

E

Egg Coffee (Scandinavia)

While Vietnam has a rich, thick, and creamy version of the egg coffee, cà phê đá, the Scandinavian preparation is milder and subtler. Instead of using egg as a creamy addition to the coffee, Scandinavian egg coffee uses egg to "treat" the coffee beans to make it less bitter.

To make this, boil 9 cups of water in a saucepan or pot. While waiting for it to boil, stir 3/4 cup freshly-ground coffee (medium to coarse grind), ¼ cup water (room temperature), and 1 egg (can be the entire egg or just the white part) in a cup. This results to a soil-like mixture.

Pour the egg-coffee mixture into the pot of boiling water. Turn down the heat if needed, just so it won't boil over. Boil it for 3 minutes. The coffee grounds will bind into a single mass that floats at the top of the pan.

After 3 minutes, remove the pot of coffee from the heat, and immediately pour in 1 cup of cold water. Let it sit for 10 minutes, until the mass or lump of coffee settles to the bottom of the pot. Cold water serves as a French press as it allows the solids to settle at the bottom.

Strain the coffee and serve.

This method has scientific explanation. First, the egg helps the coffee grounds flocculate or bind together. Second, the protein in the egg binds to the polyphenols in coffee. These polyphenols produce that astringent and bitter taste in coffee. With this, the egg serves to clarify the coffee, resulting to pleasant, mild, and non-bitter coffee that still has enough body and thickness.

This method originated from the Scandinavian region, especially in Sweden and Norway. It also has reached America as well.

Eiskaffee

This is German for ice-cream coffee. It comprises of ice cream (mostly vanilla), milk and strong chilled coffee.

Ingredients

Chocolate chips/caramel or krokant

Whipped cream

2 scoops of ice cream

1 ½ quarts strong instant coffee

Instructions

After your coffee is brewed, add it to a cup and place it in a bowl full of ice. Allow the coffee to chill for about 15 minutes. Add the scoops of ice cream to a tall glass and pour in the now cold coffee. Top with whipped cream and serve!

Espressino

This is made by mixing equal parts espresso, Nutella (hazelnut cocoa spread), and milk. Cocoa powder is also added on the bottom and on top of the drink. The drink originated from Italy, where Nutella also came from. When served cold, it is called espressino freddo. Other ingredients can also be added such as whipped cream, caramel, and chocolate syrup.

Espresso Romano

This is simply a shot of espresso served with a slice of lemon on the side. It can be run all around the rim of the cup to deepen the sweetness of the espresso. It has no link to Rome or Italy despite its name.

F

Flat White

This is a coffee drink primarily from New Zealand and Australia that is prepared by pouring micro-foam (steamed milk from the bottom of a jug) over a double (60 ml) or single shot (30ml) of espresso.

The drink is served in a small ceramic (150-160ml) cup. The micro-foam results in a velvety and smooth texture and the drink can include latte art.

A cappuccino is the same as a flat white although it uses dry foam instead of micro foam. On the other hand, a latte is somehow the same as a flat white the difference being the vessel they are served in.

How to make it

Ingredients

Espresso

Velvety micro-foam

Instructions

Add a single or double shot of espresso to a ceramic cup and pour in the micro-foam.

Frappé (American)

This is a frozen coffee beverage, a coffee slush, or a coffee shake. It was accidentally invented during the International Trade Fair of Thessaloniki Greece in 1957. During the event, Nestlé representative Giannis Dritsas mixed chocolate with water to show some kids how a chocolate beverage is done. His employee, Dimitris Vakondios, wanted to drink coffee but there was no hot water available. Seeing what Dritsas did, he blended instant coffee with cold water and ice cubes. Voila! Frappe is born. Nowadays, it is one of the most popular drinks in Greece and around the world, especially during summer and hot days. See Greek Frappe Coffee for the Greek-style version.

Starbucks has a trademarked and branded version, popularly known as Frappuccino. The beverage originated from Boston coffee shop, The Coffee Connected, which was acquired by Starbucks in 1994. Starbucks then relaunched Frappuccino under its wing in 1995, and it has become a hit among coffee drinkers. Other coffee shops also offer ice-blended beverages. It can be quite expensive though especially if you are a fan and buy it regularly, so it may be a good idea to make it at home.

How to make it

To make your own frappé or ice-blended coffee at home, follow the instructions and suggestions.

Start with 1 shot of espresso or 1 to 2 tbsp. of instant coffee.

Add 3/4 cup of milk, any kind, whether fresh or evaporated, whether full-cream or skim milk or soy milk.

Alternatively, you can use 1 scoop of ice cream or 3/4 cup condensed milk or 3/4 cup of half and half, or 3/4 cup of whipping cream.

If just using milk, add 2 tbsp. vanilla ice cream.

Add 16 oz. ice cubes. You can also add a little water if the mixture is hard to blend.

Add other flavorings and toppings as desired. Usual add-ons include brown sugar, hazelnut syrup, maple syrup, chocolate chips, citrus, berries, nuts, and fruits, among others.

Blend and shake! You can use a blender, shaker, or mixer.

Serve in a glass with a drinking straw.

G

Galão

This is a Portugal hot coffee drink made of foamed milk. It is like a café au lait or a café latte, as it comes in a tall glass with about ¾ of foamed milk and ¼ of coffee. When the proportion is 1:1, the drink is called 'meia de leite', which means half of milk and it is served in a cup.

It is somewhat like a cortado but it contains a large amount of milk; the proportions are however more like a caffe latte.

How to make it

Ingredients

Sugar to taste

Three quarters milk

One quarter coffee

Instructions

Brew an espresso. Add your milk to a saucepan and bring it to a boil. Add the espresso and the boiled milk together in a tall glass and sweeten right away with sugar as desired.

Note: Instant Nescafe Galão is a great substitute if you don't have an espresso machine.

Gibraltar

Technically, gibraltar is a cup, specifically, a brand of a
line of glass cups from Ohio company Libbey. The drink
gibraltar coffee originated from San Francisco to address
the clamor for a drink that is between a macchiato and a
latte. The drink was named after that 4-oz. glass cup
where it's served.

Gommosa

This is achieved by pouring a shot of espresso over a
single medium-sized marshmallow. This results to a
thick and sweet drink. The marshmallow does not melt
fully. Rather, it sets quickly, creating a rubbery texture
that needs some chewing, hence the name Caffè
Gommosa, which means "rubbery coffee" in Italian. The
drink originated from America's Pacific Northwest.

A variation of the drink entails using smaller pieces of
marshmallows or mini-marshmallows to create a more
evenly-melted base of marshmallows, making the drink
less rubbery.

Another variation is to use longer espresso to create a
thinner drink. This variation was suggested by Caffe
Society in United Kingdom, and they call it Caffe Society
Gommosa.

Granita al Caffe Con Panna

This is a Sicilian shaved or crushed espresso with

whipped cream.

Ingredients

Freshly-brewed espresso

Granulated sugar

Heavy cream

Instructions

Stir in the sugar when the espresso is still hot. Place it in the fridge to chill until cold (to reduce freezing time).

Once it is cold, add it to a wide baking dish (something glass or ceramic). Place the dish in a freezer and freeze for about an hour then remove. Break up the ice using 2 forks.

Return to the freezer and freeze for about 2 to 3 hours until solid as you scrape after every 30 minutes with the forks.

To serve, whip the cream to soft peaks. Place a spoonful of whipped cream at the bottom of a small glass and scoop some granita on top. Top with a larger serving of cream. Use a spoon to eat.

Note: it can be served as a dessert.

Greek Frappe Coffee

Greek frappe also known as frappe coffee is an iced coffee

drink covered in foam and made from instant coffee (spray dried coffee). It is especially popular in Cyprus and Greece during summer.

How to make it

Ingredients

Coffee

Ice cubes

Cold water

Sugar (to taste)

Instructions

The coffee can be made with either an appropriate mixer (like a hand mixer) or a cocktail mixer.

Blend 1 or 2 teaspoons of coffee, a little water and sugar to taste to form foam. Pour this into a tall glass. Add ice cubes and cold water (and evaporated milk if desired). Push in a drinking straw and enjoy.

Note:

Ice cubes are frappe tradition so they must be present.

The instant coffee contains almost no oil; just small coffee solids, molecules responsible for taste and flavor and caffeine. Once dissolved, it forms a more stable colloid compared to traditionally brewed coffee.

Guillermo

This is simply a single or double shot of steaming espresso drained over slices of lime. It can also be served cold on ice or with a touch of milk.

H

Helado de Café

This is coffee with hot caramel milk foam and vanilla ice cream.

How to make it

Ingredients

2 cups whipping cream

2 tablespoons instant coffee

1 can condensed milk (397 gram)

2 tablespoons water

Instructions

Beat the cream until it forms peaks and is very thick. Combine the water and the instant coffee until no lumps are visible. Add this mixture to a large bowl together with the condensed milk and mix well.

Add in about ¼ of the whipped cream and use a beater to mix well. Add in ¼ more of the cream and if it feels light, incorporate it with the rest of the whipped cream in batches using a spatula.

Add the mixture to a container or mold. Freeze the mixture overnight or for about 8 to 10 hours. Store any leftovers in a container with a lid in the freezer.

[?]

I

Indian Filter Coffee

Filter coffee also known as south Indian coffee is a delicious milky coffee made from chicory (20% to 30%) and coffee beans (70% to 80%). The regularly used coffee beans are Robusta and Arabica that are grown in the hills of Karnataka, Kerala and Tamil Nadu in India.

Out of India, the drink is prepared using a drip coffee or a filter coffee as the water passes through the coffee grounds by gravity and not under pressure.

How to make it

Ingredients

1 cup water

3 tablespoons coffee beans medium ground (powder)

1 teaspoon sugar

¾ cup milk

Instructions

Using a traditional coffee filter, bind the upper compartment on the lower compartment. Add the coffee grounds to the upper compartment and use the umbrella attachment to press down the grounds firmly. Cover with the umbrella attachment.

Boil the water and pour it over the umbrella in the upper

compartment until the water almost reaches the brim. Cover for about 3 to 4 hours until a thick coffee concoction forms in the bottom compartment.

To make the coffee, boil the milk and mix 4 to 5 tablespoons of the coffee brew with ¾ cup of milk as you adjust the coffee strength as desired. Add in the sugar (to taste).

Use a steel davara tumbler to get a frothy top by transferring the coffee between 2 tumblers 3 to 4 times until you get a frothy top. Serve in one davara and drink up.

Irish Coffee

Irish coffee is a cocktail made up of Irish whiskey, sugar and hot coffee stirred together and topped with a layer of thick cream where you are supposed to drink the coffee through the cream. Whipped cream is often used although the original recipe uses cream that hasn't been whipped.

How to make it

Ingredients

1 jigger Irish whiskey (1 ½ ounces or 3 tablespoons)

1 cup freshly brewed hot coffee

Heavy cream- slightly whipped

1 tablespoon brown sugar

[?]

Instructions

Fill a mug with hot water to heat it then empty. Pour the hot coffee into the warm mug up to ¾ full and add in the brown sugar. Stir until fully dissolved then combine in the Irish whiskey. Top with a layer of heavy cream through adding it gently over the back side of a spoon. Serve while hot.

J

Jamaican Dark Rum Coffee

This is a dessert drink completely resemble Irish coffee but it is made with dark rum instead of Irish whiskey.

K

Kaffeost (Swedish Coffee Cheese)

This is a coffee cheese drink from Sweden. The traditional recipe is done by putting freshly-made pieces of cheese in a cup and pouring freshly-brewed coffee in it.

To make cheese at home from scratch, Chris Kridakorn-Odbratt and Gavin Webber suggested the following recipe.

Pour 2 liters whole milk and 60 ml heavy cream in a saucepan, and heat to lukewarm. Remove from the heat and mix in 2 tsp rennet or curdled milk. Let it rest for 30 to 40 minutes until the liquid has curdled or solidified. Put back on pan to heat to lukewarm, stirring gently, guiding the curdled cheese toward the center of the pan.

Strain it using cheese cloth, pressing out as much whey or liquid as possible. Put cheese in a well-greased baking pan and bake in preheated oven (200 degrees Celsius) until browned. Cool by wrapping in aluminum foil.

Once cooled, your homemade cheese is now ready for your kaffeost.

Kopi Luwak

This is also known as civet coffee and it is the world's most expensive and less produced coffee. The coffee berries of kopi luwak are basically beans that have been consumed by an Asian Palm Civet or other civets then passed through their digestive tracts.

The civet eats the coffee beans because of their fleshy pulp. When they are in the stomach, the beans absorb the proteolytic enzymes, which make more free amino acids and shorter peptides.

Once the beans pass through the intestines, they are defecated but they keep their shape. After being gathered, serious washing, sun drying, roasting lightly and brewing, they yield a savory coffee that is much less bitter and noted as the most expensive coffee worldwide.

How to make it

Ingredients

Kopi Luwak coffee

Water

Instructions

Heat water on the stove then grind your coffee to a coarse grind—not too fine such that it passes right through the filter. Add the ground coffee into the French press coffeemaker. Once the water boils, turn off the stove and let it sit or about 45 seconds so that it can stop boiling. Pour as much hot water as you would want coffee into the ground kopi luwak in the coffeemaker.

Use a plastic soon to stir then use the lid to cover the French press; have the plunger pulled to the top. Allow it to sit for 4 minutes- you can adjust this as desired after trying it a couple of times.

Push the plunger down slowly to the bottom to push the ground coffee to the bottom of the vessel.

Pour only the brewed coffee to a glass. Enjoy!

Kopi Tubruk

This is a coffee drink originating from Indonesia where coarse grounds are boiled together with a solid sugar forming a thick drink. It is especially popular in Java and Bali and is similar to Turkish coffee.

L

Lagrima

Lagrima is the reverse of cortado and macchiato, since coffee-milk ratio is inverted. Whereas cortado and macchiato just stain the coffee with a touch or drop of milk, lagrima stains the milk with a touch or drop of coffee. In a way, it is similar with latte.

Latte (Caffé Latte)

This can be defined as a premium coffee milk experience. It is a shot of espresso with fresh steamed milk without the foam served in a tall glass. Some like having extra espresso and some syrup to their lattes. More precisely, it is 2/3 of hot milk in a long glass added 1/3 of espresso.

How to make it

Ingredients

2 cups milk

1 1/3 cups hot freshly brewed dark roast espresso coffee

Instructions

Add milk to saucepan and heat over medium low heat. Use a wire whisk and whisk briskly to create foam.

Brew espresso and add to 4 cups. Add in the milk to the espresso making sure you hold back the foam using a spoon (you can spoon back the foam on top).

This makes 4 cups of lattes.

The recipe calls for full cream milk to achieve the creamy consistency that cow's butterfat provides, but other types of milk can also be used. People use other types of milk for health reasons, or perhaps as a matter of taste, as there are some people who do not like the mouthfeel and taste of butterfat in full cream cow's milk. If skim or nonfat milk is used, it is called skinny latte. If soy milk is used, it is called soy latte. If eggnog is added, you know the drill, it's called eggnog latte. You can also use almond milk, low-fat milk, buttermilk, and other types of dairy and non-dairy milk.

Liqueur Coffee

There are many types of liqueur coffee. You can add your liqueur of choice to any preparation of coffee to get your caffeine and alcohol fix. Here are some tried and tested combinations.

- With amaretto: *Italian Classico*
- With bourbon: *American coffee*
- With brandy: *Brandy Coffee, Parisienne Coffee, French Coffee, Cafe Royale*
- With gin: *English Coffee*
- With Grand Marnier: *French Coffee*
- With grappa or sambuca: *Caffè Corretto*
- With rum: *Calypso Coffee, Spanish Coffee, Jamaican Coffee, Shin Coffee, Australian Coffee (with Bundaberg rum)*

- With schnapps: *German Coffee, Kaffekask*
- With vodka: *Russian Coffee, Karsk*
- With whisky: *Whisky Coffee, Gaelic Coffee Highland Coffee or Cup o' Evening (Scotch whiskey), Irish Coffee (Irish whiskey), Irish Cream Coffee (with Irish cream), Bailey's Coffee or Sultan Special Coffee (with brand Baileys)*

Long Black

This is used interchangeably with Americano, but they are different. Americano is done by pouring hot water into espresso, while Long Black is done by pouring espresso in hot water. This process retains the crema, is less voluminous, and has stronger flavor. This method is common in Australia and New Zealand. When you go to coffee shop chains from these regions, do not look for Americano, look instead for long black.

M

Mocha or Mochaccino

Caffe mocha is simply a latte with cocoa or chocolate syrup. It's made up of equal parts of steamed milk, espresso, whipped cream and chocolate syrup. It could also be just 1/3 of espresso, 2/3 of steamed milk and a portion of chocolate syrup. Some mochas also contain milk or dark chocolate.

Mochas can be decorated with all sorts of garnishes from cinnamon to marshmallows.

How to make it

Ingredients

1-2 cups skim milk

2/3 cup mocha powder or hot chocolate mix

Whipped cream to taste

2 tablespoons dark-roasted coffee beans

Instructions

Prepare your coffee and heat the milk on a stove making sure it doesn't burn. Pour the hot chocolate mix or mocha powder into a large mug.

Add in the skim milk to the mug and stir right away until the powder combines with the mocha syrup. Once the coffee is good to go, add it to the mug with mocha and stir.

Add some whipped cream as desired. Garnish with more powder. Drink!

N

Café noisette simply means French espresso that has very little milk in it.

O

O

Kopi O is popular in Singapore and Malaysia, which simply means coffee without any milk; it is basically plain dark coffee. Sugar is usually added to this coffee drink. Kopi O is similar to regular black coffee.

P

Palazzo

This is a variant of an iced coffee quote popular in Southern California. It is just 2 shots of espresso chilled just after brewing and then mixed with sweetened cream. It is usually made using a Moka pot.

Panna

Famously referred to as espresso con panna, this is simply double or single shots espresso that has whipped cream.

Q

Quad

This means 4 shots of espresso. Definitely not for the faint of heart!

R

Red Eye

This is an American-style cup of drip brewed coffee intensified by adding one shot of espresso. If two shots of espresso are added, it is called Black Eye. If three shots of espresso are added, it is aptly called Dead Eye. Starbucks and other coffee shops also call this ultimate caffeinated coffee drink with triple shot espresso as Green Eye or Triple Death. Meanwhile, Caffè Tobio has equal parts coffee and espresso. If the brewed coffee used is decaffeinated, it is then called Lazy Eye, although people usually just call it *Red Eye using decaf.*

Red Eye, Black Eye, and Dead/Green Eye also go by the following names: Eye-Opener, Sling Blade, Shot in the Dark, Autobahn, or Hammerhead. People like this drink because the weak and watery drip coffee balances the strength and bitterness of the espresso.

Ristretto

The word ristretto means restricted in Italian! In this case, more water is used to make espresso compared to ristretto. While espresso often uses a water: coffee ratio of 1:2, ristretto uses 1:1 making it very strong.

How to make it

Making ristretto is just like making espresso but with less counting.

Start by grinding coffee free to the same grind setting that you would use for an espresso shot (moderately fine grind size).

Then fill the portafilter to suit the machine (12-14 gram portafilter for a domestic espresso machine- just fill it up to the line in the portafilter.

Next, tamp with even and firm pressure and extract 15-20mls of coffee in just 15 seconds i.e. half the standard espresso shot which usually is 30ml in 30 seconds.

You can mix it with milk and enjoy or drink it black as a sweeter tasting single ristretto.

S

Shakerato

This is just iced coffee made by shaking shots of espresso with ice cubes. The number of shots depends on how strong you want your Shakerato to be.

T

Turkish Coffee

This is coffee made through boiling roast coffee beans
(finely powdered) 2-3 times in a pot, if possible with
sugar, and served into a cup where the dregs get to
settle. The coffee has a bit of foam on top like crema on
espresso and the more the foam the better the coffee is
considered to be.

The name doesn't mean that there is a special type of
Turkish coffee bean; it simply describes the method of
brewing. It is common all around the Middle East,
Caucasus, North Africa, Balkans and in restaurants all
around the world.

V

Vienna Coffee

This is the name of a common traditional cream based coffee drink.

How to make it

It is brewed by preparing double shots of strong black espresso in a regular sized coffee cup and then infusing it with whipped cream as a replacement for sugar and milk until the cup is filled.

The cream is then twirled and, if desired, topped with chocolate sprinklings. The coffee is then drunk via the creamy top.

W

White Coffee

Ipoh white coffee is a common coffee drink, an origin of Ipoh, Perak, Malaysia.

Palm oil margarine is used to roast the coffee beans and the resulting coffee is served together with condensed milk. The drink is delicious and smooth and usually served over ice.

White Chocolate Mocha

White chocolate mocha is prepared the same way as regular mocha or mochaccino, just replace dark chocolate or milk chocolate with white chocolate, mocha powder or hot chocolate mix with white chocolate mix.

Y

Yuanyang

This is simply 'coffee with tea' and is popular in Hong Kong. It is made by mixing coffee and Hong Kong style milk tea. Initially, the coffee was served in open air food vendors (dai pai dongs) and cafes (cha chaan tengs) but now it's available in many restaurants. It can either be served hot or cold.

Its name refers to Mandarin Ducks, which in Chinese culture signify conjugal love as the birds appear in twos while the female and male aren't so similar. The same idea of these 2 different items (tea and coffee) gave the drink its name.

How to make it

Ingredients

1 (12 ounce) can of evaporated milk (sweetened condensed milk can also work)

Sugar

3 cups of water

¼ cup black tea leaves (or six black tea bags, remove the strings)

3 cups strong coffee

Instructions

Let the water boil then add in the tea leaves or the tea bags and let simmer for about 3 minutes. Add in the milk and stir then simmer for 3 more minutes. Add in the coffee and stir then add sugar to taste and stir again. Strain.

Serve chilled over some ice or hot.

Yemen Mocha Coffee

This type of mocha does not contain chocolate, but tastes like chocolate. It is not a preparation but a variant of Arabica coffee bean. You can prepare it like you would prepare other types or variants of coffee beans. However, given its unique taste profile, it is best consumed black or with minimal add-ons only.

Yemen Mocha Coffee grows in Moka, Yemen. It is also cultivated in Saudi Arabia and some parts of Ethiopia.

Yemen Mocha Coffee can be quite difficult to source, and it is best to do research to ensure that you are buying authentic mocha beans and not just mocha-flavored or chocolate-flavored beans. Otherwise, just stick with the regular mocha preparation, or experiment with other styles such as Black Tux and Red Tux.

THANK YOU FOR READING!

the endless ways through which you can make your coffee to have a unique taste/flavor and look every single time. You don't have to visit coffee shops for the exotic coffee that they have when you have this book. And even if you do, you can at least understand what all those names on the menu mean.

Now is your turn to take action i.e. start preparing any of the coffee we've learned in the book.

If you found the book interesting, can you recommend it to other people? You can do that by leaving a review on Amazon.

Simply click this link to leave a review for this book on Amazon!

Thank you and good luck!

SETH MARTIN

73425588R00057

Made in the USA
Lexington, KY
09 December 2017